Securing the Connected World: Cybersecurity in the Age of Digital Sovereignty

ROBERTO MIGUEL RODRIGUEZ

Copyright Page

TITLE: Securing the Connected World: Cybersecurity in the Age of Digital Sovereignty

1ST Edition

ISBN: 9798223666028

Table of Contents

Securing the Connected World: Cybersecurity in the Age of Digital Sovereignty

By Roberto Miguel Rodriguez

Chapter 1: The New Frontiers: Battles for Digital Sovereignty in a Connected World

The Evolution of Digital Sovereignty

In today's interconnected world, the concept of digital sovereignty has emerged as a critical issue that demands attention from politicians, legislators, scholars, educators, and the public alike. This subchapter explores the evolution of digital sovereignty, shedding light on the various aspects that have shaped its development and importance.

The New Frontiers: Battles for Digital Sovereignty in a Connected World

The rapid advancement of technology has given rise to new frontiers where battles for digital sovereignty are being fought. As nations grapple with the complexities of cybersecurity and data protection, it is crucial to understand the evolving landscape and the challenges it presents.

Cybersecurity in the Age of Digital Sovereignty

The concept of digital sovereignty intersects with cybersecurity, as nations strive to protect their digital assets and critical infrastructure from cyber threats. This subchapter explores the key cybersecurity challenges faced by nations in the age of digital sovereignty and the strategies employed to mitigate risks.

National Data Protection Regulations and Digital Sovereignty

National data protection regulations play a pivotal role in shaping digital sovereignty. This section delves into the importance of robust data protection laws and the implications they have on a nation's ability to safeguard its citizens' data and maintain control over its digital domain.

Geopolitics of Internet Governance and Digital Sovereignty

Internet governance has become a battleground for asserting digital sovereignty. This subchapter examines the geopolitical dynamics at play, the role of international organizations, and the implications for nations seeking to protect their interests in cyberspace.

Economic Implications of Digital Sovereignty in International Trade

Digital sovereignty has significant economic implications, particularly in the context of international trade. This section explores the delicate balance between protecting national interests and fostering global economic cooperation in the digital age.

Privacy and Surveillance in the Context of Digital Sovereignty

As nations assert their digital sovereignty, questions surrounding privacy and surveillance arise. This subchapter delves into the ethical and legal considerations surrounding surveillance practices, the impact on individual privacy, and the need for transparent and accountable frameworks.

Digital Sovereignty and the Future of Cloud Computing

Cloud computing has revolutionized the way data is stored and accessed, but it also raises concerns about digital sovereignty. This section explores the challenges and opportunities for nations in maintaining control over their data in an increasingly cloud-dependent world.

Cultural Preservation and Digital Sovereignty

The digital age presents unique challenges to cultural preservation. This subchapter examines the role of digital sovereignty in protecting cultural heritage and ensuring diverse cultural expressions thrive in the face of digital globalization.

Digital Sovereignty and the Role of Artificial Intelligence

As artificial intelligence continues to advance, questions of digital sovereignty arise. This section explores the implications of AI on national interests, the need for ethical AI frameworks, and the role of digital sovereignty in harnessing the potential of AI for societal benefit.

Digital Rights and Digital Sovereignty

Digital sovereignty is closely intertwined with digital rights. This subchapter examines the relationship between the two, exploring how digital sovereignty can protect and promote individual rights in a digital world.

Ethical Considerations in the Battles for Digital Sovereignty

The battles for digital sovereignty raise important ethical considerations. This final section discusses the ethical dilemmas faced by nations, the need for responsible digital governance, and the importance of ethical frameworks in shaping the future of digital sovereignty.

In conclusion, the evolution of digital sovereignty is a complex and multifaceted issue that demands attention from various stakeholders. This subchapter provides a comprehensive overview of the key aspects related to digital sovereignty, shedding light on its significance in an increasingly connected world.

The Impact of Global Interconnectivity

In today's interconnected world, global interconnectivity has revolutionized the way we live, work, and interact with one another. The digital age has brought about unprecedented opportunities and challenges, particularly in the realm of cybersecurity. This subchapter explores the profound impact of global interconnectivity on various aspects of our society and the battles for digital sovereignty that have emerged as a result.

One of the key areas affected by global interconnectivity is national data protection regulations and digital sovereignty. As countries strive to protect their citizens' data and maintain control over their digital infrastructure, tensions arise between the need for global cooperation and the desire for national sovereignty. Finding the right balance is crucial to safeguarding individual privacy and maintaining trust in the digital realm.

Furthermore, the geopolitics of internet governance and digital sovereignty have become increasingly complex. The power dynamics between nations and the struggle for influence over global internet governance bodies have significant implications for cybersecurity and the protection of digital rights. Understanding these dynamics is essential for policymakers and legislators as they navigate the evolving landscape of digital sovereignty.

Moreover, the economic implications of digital sovereignty in international trade cannot be overlooked. As countries assert their control over data flows and digital infrastructure, trade barriers may emerge, impacting economic integration and global commerce. Balancing the economic benefits of digital globalization with the need to protect national interests poses a significant challenge for policymakers.

In the context of digital sovereignty, privacy and surveillance have become pressing concerns. Striking a balance between individual privacy rights and the need for national security in an interconnected world is a complex task. Policymakers must grapple with ethical considerations and develop robust frameworks to safeguard privacy while ensuring effective surveillance measures.

The future of cloud computing is also deeply intertwined with digital sovereignty. As countries assert control over their digital infrastructure, questions arise about the future of cloud computing and data storage. Policymakers must consider the implications of digital sovereignty on the global cloud market and develop strategies to protect national interests without stifling innovation.

Furthermore, cultural preservation in the digital age is a significant concern. As global interconnectivity increases, the preservation of cultural heritage and diversity faces new challenges. Policymakers must address these challenges to ensure that digital sovereignty does not undermine cultural preservation efforts.

Artificial intelligence (AI) also plays a crucial role in the battles for digital sovereignty. As AI technologies advance, issues such as algorithmic bias and control over AI systems become central to discussions on digital sovereignty. Policymakers and scholars must grapple with the ethical implications of AI and develop regulations that protect individual rights while fostering innovation.

In conclusion, global interconnectivity has far-reaching implications for various aspects of our society. The battles for digital sovereignty require careful consideration of national interests, privacy rights, economic implications, and ethical considerations. Policymakers, legislators, scholars, educators, and the public must engage in these discussions to shape the future of cybersecurity in the age of digital sovereignty.

Challenges and Opportunities in the Age of Digital Sovereignty

In today's interconnected world, the concept of digital sovereignty has emerged as a critical issue that demands attention from policymakers, scholars, educators, and the general public. As the internet becomes increasingly pervasive in all aspects of our lives, it is essential to understand the challenges and opportunities that arise in this new era.

One of the key challenges in the age of digital sovereignty is the battle for control over the flow of information and data. With the rise of national data protection regulations, countries are asserting their right to govern the data that traverses their borders. This has significant implications for businesses operating in the global marketplace, as they must navigate a complex web of regulations to ensure compliance while maintaining seamless cross-border operations.

Moreover, the geopolitics of internet governance also play a crucial role in shaping digital sovereignty. Different countries have different visions for how the internet should be governed, leading to tensions and conflicts. It is imperative for policymakers to engage in international discussions and negotiations to establish common ground and ensure a globally connected digital ecosystem.

The economic implications of digital sovereignty in international trade cannot be ignored either. While protecting national interests and data privacy is crucial, excessive regulations and barriers can hinder the free flow of data and impede innovation and economic growth. Policymakers must strike a delicate balance between protecting sovereignty and fostering a conducive environment for international trade and collaboration.

Additionally, privacy and surveillance are important considerations in the context of digital sovereignty. Striking the right balance between privacy rights and national security is a complex task that requires careful deliberation and robust legal frameworks. It is essential to protect individual privacy while ensuring that governments have the necessary tools and capabilities to combat cyber threats and maintain public safety.

Furthermore, the future of cloud computing and its relationship with digital sovereignty is an area that demands attention. As more data is stored and processed in the cloud, questions arise about who has ultimate control and ownership over that data. Policymakers must address these concerns to ensure that individuals and businesses have confidence in the security and privacy of their data.

Cultural preservation is another important aspect of digital sovereignty. As more aspects of our cultural heritage are digitized, it is essential to protect and preserve these artifacts in a manner that respects national and cultural identity. Policies must be developed to ensure that digital platforms and companies do not undermine or dilute cultural diversity.

The role of artificial intelligence (AI) in the battles for digital sovereignty also deserves careful consideration. As AI becomes increasingly integrated into our lives, questions arise about who controls the algorithms and decision-making processes. Policymakers must address ethical concerns and ensure that AI systems are transparent, accountable, and aligned with societal values.

Finally, digital rights and ethical considerations are paramount in the age of digital sovereignty. It is essential to protect individuals' rights to access information, express themselves online, and maintain control over their personal data. Policymakers must develop robust legal frameworks that safeguard these rights while promoting responsible and ethical behavior in the digital realm.

In conclusion, the age of digital sovereignty presents both challenges and opportunities for policymakers, scholars, educators, and the public. By addressing issues such as national data protection regulations, geopolitics of internet governance, economic implications, privacy and surveillance, cloud computing, cultural preservation, AI, digital rights, and ethical considerations, we can collectively shape a secure and connected world that respects individual sovereignty and promotes global collaboration.

Chapter 2: Cybersecurity in the Age of Digital Sovereignty

Understanding Cybersecurity Threats

In today's interconnected world, cybersecurity threats have become a pressing concern for individuals, businesses, and governments alike. This subchapter aims to provide a comprehensive understanding of these threats and their implications in the context of digital sovereignty.

Cybersecurity threats encompass a wide range of malicious activities that seek to exploit vulnerabilities in digital systems. These threats can come in various forms, including malware, phishing attacks, ransomware, and distributed denial-of-service (DDoS) attacks. Understanding these threats is crucial for policymakers, legislators, scholars, educators, and the general public to effectively address the challenges posed by the digital age.

The New Frontiers: Battles for Digital Sovereignty in a Connected World explores the geopolitical landscape of internet governance and the need for national data protection regulations. As countries strive to protect their citizens' data and assert their digital sovereignty, cybersecurity threats pose a significant obstacle. This subchapter delves into the intricate relationship between cybersecurity and digital sovereignty, highlighting the importance of robust cybersecurity measures to safeguard national interests and preserve individual privacy.

Moreover, the economic implications of digital sovereignty in international trade cannot be overlooked. As countries implement data localization requirements and impose restrictions on cross-border data flows, businesses face new challenges in maintaining secure and efficient operations. This subchapter sheds light on the economic considerations surrounding cybersecurity and the potential impact on international trade.

Privacy and surveillance are also critical aspects of cybersecurity in the context of digital sovereignty. Balancing the need for surveillance to ensure national security with the protection of individuals' privacy rights is a complex task. This subchapter examines the delicate balance between privacy and surveillance, exploring potential frameworks and solutions to address these concerns.

Furthermore, the emergence of cloud computing and artificial intelligence (AI) technologies has profound implications for digital sovereignty. This subchapter explores the future of cloud computing in the context of digital sovereignty, discussing the challenges and opportunities presented by these technologies.

Lastly, ethical considerations play a crucial role in the battles for digital sovereignty. As governments and businesses navigate the complex landscape of cybersecurity, it is essential to uphold ethical principles and respect human rights. This subchapter delves into the ethical considerations surrounding digital sovereignty, emphasizing the need for responsible decision-making and collaboration to ensure a secure and inclusive digital future.

Understanding cybersecurity threats is essential for policymakers, legislators, scholars, educators, and the public. By comprehending the intricacies of these threats, stakeholders can develop effective strategies and policies to protect national interests, preserve individual privacy, and foster a secure digital environment.

The Role of Government in Ensuring Cybersecurity

In today's interconnected world, where the internet has become an integral part of our daily lives, the need for robust cybersecurity measures has become paramount. As technology advances and more critical infrastructure relies on digital systems, the role of government in ensuring cybersecurity has never been more crucial. This subchapter explores the various ways in which governments can play a proactive role in safeguarding their nations against cyber threats.

Governments have a responsibility to protect their citizens, and this extends to the digital realm. One of the primary roles of government in ensuring cybersecurity is the establishment and enforcement of national data protection regulations. These regulations provide a framework for organizations to follow, setting minimum standards for the protection of personal and sensitive information. By enforcing these regulations, governments can hold organizations accountable for any breaches and ensure that proper cybersecurity measures are in place.

Furthermore, governments are tasked with the geopolitics of internet governance and digital sovereignty. In an era where nations are vying for control over the internet, governments must navigate the complexities of international relations and work towards establishing a secure and stable cyberspace. This involves participating in global forums, negotiating treaties, and collaborating with other nations to develop shared cybersecurity objectives.

The economic implications of digital sovereignty in international trade cannot be overlooked. Governments play a pivotal role in creating an enabling environment for businesses to thrive while also ensuring that cybersecurity is not compromised. By investing in research and development, fostering innovation, and providing incentives for businesses to adopt cybersecurity best practices, governments can create a resilient digital ecosystem that promotes economic growth and protects national interests.

Privacy and surveillance are also critical considerations in the context of digital sovereignty. Governments must strike a delicate balance between protecting citizens' privacy rights and maintaining the ability to detect and prevent cyber threats. Transparent and accountable surveillance programs, coupled with robust privacy regulations, can help achieve this balance.

Moreover, as the world becomes increasingly reliant on cloud computing, governments must safeguard their digital sovereignty. By establishing regulations and standards for cloud service providers, governments can ensure that sensitive national data is stored and processed within their borders, reducing the risk of unauthorized access or data breaches.

The role of artificial intelligence (AI) in cybersecurity cannot be undermined. Governments must invest in AI research and development to enhance their cybersecurity capabilities. AI-powered systems can detect and respond to cyber threats in real-time, providing governments with the tools necessary to stay one step ahead of cybercriminals.

Lastly, ethical considerations must be at the forefront of the battles for digital sovereignty. Governments must ensure that their cybersecurity efforts do not infringe upon the rights and freedoms of their citizens. This requires transparency, accountability, and ongoing dialogue with stakeholders, including scholars, educators, and the public.

In conclusion, the role of government in ensuring cybersecurity is multifaceted and essential in today's interconnected world. By enacting national data protection regulations, participating in global internet governance discussions, promoting cybersecurity in international trade, protecting privacy rights, safeguarding digital sovereignty, investing in AI research, and upholding ethical standards, governments can create a secure and resilient digital environment for their citizens.

Collaborative Efforts in Combating Cybersecurity Threats

In today's interconnected world, the battle against cybersecurity threats has become a global concern. The rapid advancement of technology and the increasing reliance on digital infrastructure have made countries vulnerable to cyberattacks, putting the security and sovereignty of nations at risk. To effectively combat these threats, collaborative efforts among various stakeholders are crucial.

Politicians, legislators, scholars, educators, and the general public all have a role to play in this fight. It is imperative for them to understand the implications of cybersecurity threats and work together to develop comprehensive strategies to protect national interests and ensure digital sovereignty.

The new frontiers of battles for digital sovereignty highlight the need for international cooperation. Nations must come together to share threat intelligence, best practices, and resources to enhance their collective defense capabilities. Collaborative platforms should be established to facilitate information sharing and the development of joint defense mechanisms.

To strengthen cybersecurity, national data protection regulations should be harmonized. This will not only protect citizens' privacy but also ensure that data is securely stored and transmitted across borders. The development of international standards and frameworks can help create a unified approach to cybersecurity, making it more difficult for cybercriminals to exploit vulnerabilities.

The geopolitics of internet governance and digital sovereignty play a critical role in shaping cybersecurity efforts. Countries must work together to address issues related to jurisdiction, sovereignty, and cross-border cyber threats. Diplomatic channels should be utilized to foster cooperation and resolve disputes related to cybercrime.

The economic implications of digital sovereignty in international trade cannot be ignored. Collaborative efforts should focus on promoting a secure digital environment that enables innovation and economic growth. International trade agreements should incorporate cybersecurity provisions to protect businesses and consumers from cyber threats.

Privacy and surveillance are important considerations in the context of digital sovereignty. Collaborative efforts should aim to strike a balance between the need for national security and individuals' privacy rights. Transparent and accountable surveillance practices must be implemented to ensure the protection of civil liberties.

As the future of cloud computing unfolds, collaborative efforts must be made to address the security risks associated with cloud-based services. Nations should work together to establish robust security standards and protocols that safeguard data stored in the cloud.

Cultural preservation is another aspect of digital sovereignty that requires collaborative efforts. Nations should cooperate to protect their cultural heritage from cyber threats and digital exploitation. Collaborative platforms can be created to promote the exchange of knowledge and expertise in this area.

The role of artificial intelligence (AI) in digital sovereignty cannot be underestimated. Collaborative efforts should focus on developing ethical AI frameworks that prioritize privacy, security, and human rights. Joint research and development initiatives can help nations leverage AI technology while minimizing the risks associated with it.

Digital rights must be protected in the battles for digital sovereignty. Collaborative efforts should aim to establish international norms and standards that safeguard individuals' rights to freedom of expression, access to information, and privacy.

Ethical considerations should guide collaborative efforts in the battles for digital sovereignty. Nations must work together to develop ethical guidelines for cybersecurity practices and ensure that the deployment of defensive measures does not infringe upon human rights or international laws.

In conclusion, collaborative efforts are essential in combating cybersecurity threats and securing the connected world. Politicians, legislators, scholars, educators, and the public must work together to develop comprehensive strategies that protect national interests, preserve cultural heritage, and safeguard individual rights in the age of digital sovereignty. By fostering international cooperation, sharing knowledge, and harmonizing regulations, we can create a safer and more secure digital environment for all.

Chapter 3: National Data Protection Regulations and Digital Sovereignty

The Importance of National Data Protection Regulations

In today's interconnected world, where data flows seamlessly across borders and cyber threats are ever-present, the need for robust national data protection regulations cannot be overstated. These regulations play a crucial role in safeguarding the privacy and security of individuals, promoting trust in digital services, and upholding the principles of digital sovereignty. This subchapter will delve into the significance of national data protection regulations in the context of digital sovereignty and its implications across various domains.

The New Frontiers: Battles for Digital Sovereignty in a Connected World

In the era of digital sovereignty, nations are grappling with new frontiers that emerge from the interconnectedness of the digital world. National data protection regulations serve as a critical tool for governments to assert their control over data and protect their citizens from potential harm.

Cybersecurity in the Age of Digital Sovereignty

National data protection regulations form an integral part of a comprehensive cybersecurity strategy. By establishing clear guidelines and standards for data protection, governments can fortify their cyber defenses and enhance resilience against cyber threats. These regulations also enable the sharing of threat intelligence and foster international cooperation in combating cybercrime.

Geopolitics of Internet Governance and Digital Sovereignty

National data protection regulations contribute to the geopolitical dynamics of internet governance. They empower nations to assert control over their digital infrastructure, safeguard national interests, and protect sensitive information from foreign interference. These regulations also shape the global landscape of internet governance by influencing international norms and standards.

Economic Implications of Digital Sovereignty in International Trade

National data protection regulations have significant economic implications in the realm of international trade. They provide a framework for secure data flows, bolster consumer confidence, and facilitate cross-border data transfers while ensuring compliance with privacy and security requirements. Harmonizing these regulations can foster trust among trading partners and spur economic growth.

Privacy and Surveillance in the Context of Digital Sovereignty

National data protection regulations strike a delicate balance between privacy and surveillance. They safeguard individuals' right to privacy by imposing restrictions on data collection, processing, and storage while allowing governments to conduct lawful surveillance activities for national security purposes. These regulations ensure transparency, accountability, and protection against unlawful surveillance practices.

Digital sovereignty is a multifaceted concept that encompasses a wide range of issues, including cloud computing, artificial intelligence, digital rights, and ethical considerations. National data protection regulations play a pivotal role in shaping the future of these domains, ensuring that technological advancements align with societal values, ethical standards, and national interests.

In conclusion, national data protection regulations are of paramount importance in the age of digital sovereignty. They serve as the foundation for secure and trusted digital ecosystems, bolster cybersecurity, protect individual privacy, and facilitate international cooperation. Policymakers, legislators, scholars, educators, and the public must recognize the significance of these regulations and work together to create a harmonized global framework that upholds the principles of digital sovereignty and safeguards the connected world.

Balancing Data Privacy and National Security

In the digital age, the need to balance data privacy and national security has become increasingly complex. As the world becomes more interconnected, governments and individuals alike find themselves grappling with the challenges of protecting sensitive information while ensuring the safety and well-being of their citizens. This subchapter explores the delicate balance between data privacy and national security, examining the implications for policymakers, legislators, scholars, educators, and the general public.

The New Frontiers: Battles for Digital Sovereignty in a Connected World

As nations compete for dominance in the global digital landscape, the concept of digital sovereignty takes center stage. This subchapter delves into the new frontiers of battles for digital sovereignty, exploring how data privacy and national security intersect in this rapidly evolving landscape. It examines the geopolitical implications, challenges, and opportunities that arise as countries strive to assert their control over internet governance and secure their digital borders.

Cybersecurity in the Age of Digital Sovereignty

The rise of cyber threats has necessitated a reevaluation of traditional security paradigms. This subchapter discusses the evolving role of cybersecurity in the age of digital sovereignty. It explores the strategies, policies, and technologies required to ensure the protection of critical infrastructure, sensitive data, and national interests, while respecting individual privacy rights.

National Data Protection Regulations and Digital Sovereignty

In an era where data is the new currency, national data protection regulations play a pivotal role in safeguarding citizen rights and national security. This subchapter examines the intersection between these regulations and the notion of digital sovereignty. It explores the challenges of harmonizing global data protection standards and the implications for international trade, diplomacy, and individual privacy.

Privacy and Surveillance in the Context of Digital Sovereignty

The trade-off between privacy and surveillance has become a contentious issue in the digital sovereignty debate. This subchapter explores the ethical, legal, and social implications of surveillance practices in the context of digital sovereignty. It examines the delicate balance between protecting individual privacy rights and ensuring national security in an increasingly interconnected world.

Digital Sovereignty and the Future of Cloud Computing

Cloud computing has revolutionized the way data is stored and accessed. However, concerns about data privacy and security have raised questions about the future of cloud computing in the context of digital sovereignty. This subchapter delves into the challenges and opportunities of harnessing the potential of cloud computing while safeguarding national interests and individual privacy.

As the world grapples with the complexities of digital sovereignty, various considerations come into play. This subchapter explores the ethical dimensions of the battles for digital sovereignty, examining the implications for digital rights and individual freedoms. It discusses the importance of upholding ethical principles in the pursuit of national security and data privacy.

In conclusion, the delicate balance between data privacy and national security is a critical issue in today's interconnected world. This subchapter provides insights and analysis for policymakers, legislators, scholars, educators, and the general public to better understand the challenges and opportunities that arise in the pursuit of digital sovereignty. By examining the various dimensions of this complex issue, it aims to foster informed discussions and shape policies that strike the right balance between protecting individual privacy rights and ensuring national security.

Case Studies: Successful National Data Protection Regulations

In the age of digital sovereignty, the battle for protecting data and ensuring cybersecurity has become paramount. National data protection regulations play a crucial role in safeguarding citizens' privacy, promoting trust, and fostering economic growth in the digital era. This subchapter explores the success stories of countries that have implemented effective data protection regulations, highlighting their impact on various aspects of society.

One exemplary case study is the European Union's General Data Protection Regulation (GDPR). Introduced in 2018, the GDPR revolutionized data protection by establishing a comprehensive framework for the collection, processing, and storage of personal data. Its extraterritorial reach and stringent penalties for non-compliance have incentivized businesses worldwide to prioritize data protection. The GDPR has empowered citizens with greater control over their personal information, enhancing trust and privacy in the digital realm.

Singapore provides another noteworthy example with its Personal Data Protection Act (PDPA). This legislation governs the collection, use, and disclosure of personal data by organizations. The PDPA's key strength lies in its flexible approach, allowing businesses to adapt their practices while ensuring the protection of individuals' data. Singapore's robust data protection regime has not only boosted consumer confidence but also positioned the country as a hub for data-driven innovation and international business.

Closer to home, the United States has witnessed remarkable progress with the California Consumer Privacy Act (CCPA). Enacted in 2020, the CCPA grants California residents extensive rights over their personal data, including the right to know, delete, and opt-out of data sharing. Its implementation has prompted companies to improve their data handling practices, promoting transparency and accountability. The CCPA has set a precedent for other states and countries, inspiring similar legislation worldwide.

These case studies demonstrate that successful national data protection regulations are multifaceted in their impact. They not only protect individual privacy but also foster innovation, create a level playing field for businesses, and bolster international trust. Policymakers, legislators, and scholars should take inspiration from these success stories when formulating data protection regulations tailored to their specific contexts.

Furthermore, it is essential to recognize the interconnected nature of data protection and digital sovereignty. Robust data protection regulations are a cornerstone of maintaining digital sovereignty, as they empower nations to assert control over their citizens' data and protect against external threats. By establishing comprehensive frameworks, countries can navigate the geopolitical challenges of internet governance while preserving their cultural values and national interests.

As we delve deeper into the future of cloud computing, artificial intelligence, and digital rights, ethical considerations must remain at the forefront. National data protection regulations should strike a balance between privacy and surveillance, ensuring that citizens' rights are upheld while enabling law enforcement and counterterrorism efforts. By addressing these complex ethical dilemmas, policymakers can navigate the battles for digital sovereignty with integrity and foresight.

In conclusion, successful national data protection regulations are crucial for securing the connected world in the age of digital sovereignty. The case studies of the GDPR, PDPA, and CCPA illustrate the positive impact of such regulations on privacy, innovation, and international trust. By learning from these success stories, policymakers, legislators, and scholars can formulate effective data protection frameworks that safeguard citizens' privacy while fostering economic growth and preserving cultural values. The battles for digital sovereignty require a multidimensional approach, encompassing geopolitics, ethics, and the future of technology. Only through comprehensive and forward-thinking strategies can we ensure a secure and prosperous connected world.

Chapter 4: Geopolitics of Internet Governance and Digital Sovereignty

The Power Dynamics in Internet Governance

In the age of digital sovereignty, the battles for control over the connected world have intensified. At the heart of these battles lies the power dynamics in internet governance, a complex web of relationships between governments, corporations, and individuals that shape the future of our interconnected society.

The power dynamics in internet governance are multifaceted and have far-reaching implications for various stakeholders. Politicians and legislators play a pivotal role in shaping policies and regulations that govern the internet. Their decisions have the power to either protect or undermine digital sovereignty, the ability of a nation to govern its own digital space.

Scholars and educators also have a critical role to play in understanding and analyzing the power dynamics in internet governance. By studying the intricate relationships between governments, corporations, and individuals, they can provide valuable insights into the challenges and opportunities that arise in the digital era.

For the public, understanding the power dynamics in internet governance is essential in navigating the digital landscape. It empowers individuals to make informed decisions about their online presence, privacy, and security. Furthermore, it encourages active participation in shaping the policies that govern the internet, ensuring that the voices of the public are heard.

The power dynamics in internet governance intersect with various niches within the broader theme of digital sovereignty. National data protection regulations, for example, are a manifestation of a country's effort to assert control over its digital assets. These regulations reflect the delicate balance between protecting citizens' privacy and enabling innovation and economic growth.

The geopolitics of internet governance also play a significant role in shaping power dynamics. As countries vie for influence and control over the internet, alliances are formed, and conflicts arise. The economic implications of digital sovereignty in international trade are also at stake, as countries seek to protect their domestic industries and ensure fair competition in the global marketplace.

Privacy and surveillance are central to the power dynamics in internet governance. Balancing the need for security with the protection of individual rights is a delicate task. The battles for digital sovereignty raise important ethical considerations, as the actions of governments and corporations have far-reaching consequences for the rights and freedoms of individuals.

The future of cloud computing, the role of artificial intelligence, digital rights, and cultural preservation are all intricately linked to the power dynamics in internet governance. Understanding these dynamics is crucial in ensuring that the digital era is characterized by inclusivity, transparency, and respect for individual rights.

In conclusion, the power dynamics in internet governance are complex and multifaceted. Understanding these dynamics is essential for politicians, legislators, scholars, educators, and the public. By analyzing and navigating the power dynamics, we can collectively shape a future that upholds digital sovereignty, protects individual rights, and fosters innovation and economic growth in the connected world.

National Control vs. Global Cooperation in Internet Governance

The rapid growth of the internet and the ever-increasing interconnectedness of our world have brought about a complex set of challenges for policymakers and governments. One of the most pressing issues is the question of who should be in control of internet governance – should it be left to individual nations or should there be global cooperation?

In this subchapter, we will explore the tensions between national control and global cooperation in internet governance and delve into the implications for various stakeholders. This topic is of utmost importance to politicians, legislators, scholars, educators, and the general public, as it directly affects the way we navigate the digital realm and safeguard our rights and interests.

The New Frontiers: Battles for Digital Sovereignty in a Connected World

As the world becomes increasingly interconnected, battles for digital sovereignty are emerging as new frontiers in international relations. Nations are grappling with the question of how to protect their citizens' data and maintain control over their digital infrastructure while still participating in the global digital economy.

Cybersecurity in the Age of Digital Sovereignty

With cyber threats on the rise, the need for robust cybersecurity measures is paramount. However, the question of who should be responsible for ensuring cybersecurity has become a point of contention. Should it be the responsibility of individual nations, or should there be a global framework for cooperation and information sharing?

National Data Protection Regulations and Digital Sovereignty

Data protection regulations play a crucial role in safeguarding individuals' privacy and ensuring the security of their personal information. However, the implementation of these regulations can vary greatly from one country to another. This raises questions about how national data protection regulations impact digital sovereignty and whether there is a need for global standards in this area.

Geopolitics of Internet Governance and Digital Sovereignty

Internet governance has become a geopolitical battleground, with nations vying for control and influence over the digital realm. This raises concerns about the potential for internet fragmentation and the impact it may have on global connectivity and access to information.

Economic Implications of Digital Sovereignty in International Trade

Digital sovereignty has significant implications for international trade. Nations that prioritize national control over internet governance may impose restrictions on cross-border data flows, potentially hindering digital trade and innovation. This raises important questions about striking a balance between national interests and the benefits of a globalized digital economy.

Privacy and Surveillance in the Context of Digital Sovereignty

The tension between privacy and surveillance is a key aspect of the national control vs. global cooperation debate. Striking the right balance between ensuring national security and protecting individuals' privacy rights is a delicate task that requires careful consideration and collaboration at both the national and international levels.

Digital Sovereignty and the Future of Cloud Computing

Cloud computing has revolutionized the way we store and access data. However, concerns about data sovereignty and security have led to calls for increased national control over cloud services. This subchapter will explore the implications of digital sovereignty on the future of cloud computing and the challenges it presents for international data management.

Cultural Preservation and Digital Sovereignty

Digital sovereignty also extends to the preservation and protection of cultural heritage in the digital age. Nations are grappling with how to safeguard their cultural identity and ensure the preservation of their cultural artifacts in an increasingly globalized and interconnected world.

Digital Sovereignty and the Role of Artificial Intelligence

Artificial intelligence (AI) is poised to transform various aspects of society, from healthcare to transportation. However, questions about data ownership, algorithmic transparency, and ethical considerations have prompted discussions on how to maintain control and sovereignty in the age of AI.

Digital Rights and Digital Sovereignty

The battles for digital sovereignty have significant implications for digital rights and freedoms. This subchapter will explore how the tensions between national control and global cooperation impact individuals' rights to access information, express opinions, and participate in the digital realm.

Ethical Considerations in the Battles for Digital Sovereignty

As we navigate the complex landscape of digital sovereignty, ethical considerations must guide our decision-making processes. This subchapter will delve into the ethical implications of national control vs. global cooperation in internet governance and shed light on the ethical frameworks that should inform our approach to these challenges.

In conclusion, the tensions between national control and global cooperation in internet governance have far-reaching implications for various stakeholders, including politicians, legislators, scholars, educators, and the general public. This subchapter aims to provide a comprehensive overview of the key issues at play and stimulate further discussion on how to secure the connected world in the age of digital sovereignty.

The Role of International Organizations in Internet Governance

In the age of digital sovereignty, the role of international organizations in internet governance has become increasingly crucial. As the world becomes more interconnected, ensuring the security and stability of the internet has become a global concern. This subchapter will delve into the significance of international organizations in shaping internet governance policies and regulations.

International organizations, such as the United Nations (UN), the International Telecommunication Union (ITU), and the Internet Corporation for Assigned Names and Numbers (ICANN), play a pivotal role in facilitating cooperation among nations and addressing the challenges of internet governance. These organizations provide a platform for countries to come together and develop common frameworks that promote the security, stability, and openness of the internet.

One of the primary tasks of these organizations is to establish norms and standards for internet governance. This includes addressing issues such as cybercrime, data protection, privacy, and surveillance. By developing international treaties and agreements, these organizations ensure that countries adhere to common principles and regulations, thus fostering trust and cooperation in cyberspace.

Furthermore, international organizations also serve as mediators between different stakeholders in the internet governance ecosystem. They bring together governments, private sector entities, civil society organizations, and technical experts to engage in dialogue and develop consensus-based policies. This multi-stakeholder approach ensures that the interests and concerns of all parties are taken into account, leading to more effective and inclusive internet governance frameworks.

Moreover, international organizations play a vital role in capacity building and knowledge sharing. They provide resources, training programs, and technical assistance to help countries develop their cybersecurity capabilities and enhance their understanding of internet governance issues. This is particularly important for developing nations that may face unique challenges in securing their digital infrastructure.

In conclusion, international organizations have a significant role to play in internet governance in the age of digital sovereignty. By establishing norms, facilitating dialogue, and providing capacity-building support, these organizations contribute to a safer and more secure cyberspace. It is imperative for politicians, legislators, scholars, educators, and the public to recognize the importance of international cooperation in addressing the complex challenges of internet governance and work towards strengthening the role of these organizations in shaping the future of the connected world.

Chapter 5: Economic Implications of Digital Sovereignty in International Trade

The Impact of Digital Sovereignty on Global Trade

In an increasingly interconnected world, the concept of digital sovereignty has emerged as a crucial topic of discussion. As governments and organizations grapple with the challenges and opportunities presented by the digital age, it becomes imperative to understand the impact of digital sovereignty on global trade.

Digital sovereignty refers to a nation's ability to govern its own digital infrastructure, data, and policies in a manner that aligns with its national interests and values. It encompasses a wide range of issues, including data protection regulations, internet governance, privacy, surveillance, and the ethical considerations surrounding digital rights.

The battles for digital sovereignty are the new frontiers in the global landscape, with politicians, legislators, scholars, educators, and the general public all having a stake in its outcome. The economic implications of digital sovereignty on international trade are significant. As nations assert their digital sovereignty, they may impose national data protection regulations that can impact cross-border data flows. This can have far-reaching consequences for multinational companies, as they navigate a complex landscape of varying data protection standards.

Moreover, the geopolitics of internet governance and digital sovereignty come into play. Countries vie for control and influence over the internet, leading to debates and tensions over issues such as censorship, surveillance, and cyber warfare. These geopolitical dynamics can have a profound impact on global trade, as access to digital markets and the free flow of information become contested issues.

Digital sovereignty also intersects with other domains, such as cloud computing, artificial intelligence, and cultural preservation. The future of cloud computing is closely tied to digital sovereignty, as nations seek to protect their data and infrastructure from foreign influence. Similarly, artificial intelligence raises questions about the role of digital sovereignty in shaping the development and deployment of AI technologies.

Furthermore, the battles for digital sovereignty have ethical implications. As governments and organizations assert control over their digital ecosystems, questions arise about the balance between security, privacy, and individual rights. The tension between surveillance and privacy is particularly pertinent, as governments seek to protect national security while respecting the rights of their citizens.

In conclusion, digital sovereignty has a profound impact on global trade. The economic, geopolitical, ethical, and cultural dimensions of digital sovereignty shape the interconnected world we live in. As politicians, legislators, scholars, educators, and the public engage with these issues, it is crucial to navigate the complexities of digital sovereignty to ensure a secure and prosperous future in the age of connectivity.

Trade Barriers and Protectionism in the Digital Age

In the rapidly evolving digital age, the concept of trade barriers and protectionism has taken on a new dimension. As the world becomes increasingly interconnected, the need to address issues such as cybersecurity, data protection, and digital sovereignty has become paramount. This subchapter explores the challenges and implications of trade barriers and protectionism in the digital age, shedding light on the complex landscape that policymakers, scholars, and the public must navigate.

The New Frontiers: Battles for Digital Sovereignty in a Connected World

In this subchapter, we delve into the new frontiers of battles for digital sovereignty in a connected world. As nations grapple with the tension between protecting their national interests and participating in the global digital economy, we explore the various strategies employed by governments to secure their digital sovereignty. From data localization requirements to restrictions on cross-border data flows, we examine the impact of these battles on international trade and the global digital landscape.

Cybersecurity in the Age of Digital Sovereignty

With the rise of cyber threats, ensuring cybersecurity has become a top priority for governments worldwide. In this section, we analyze how the pursuit of digital sovereignty influences cybersecurity measures. From the development of national cybersecurity frameworks to the deployment of advanced technologies, we explore how countries are strengthening their cyber defenses while simultaneously grappling with the challenges of an interconnected world.

National Data Protection Regulations and Digital Sovereignty

The protection of personal data has emerged as a critical issue in the digital age. We delve into the implications of national data protection regulations on digital sovereignty. From the European Union's General Data Protection Regulation (GDPR) to other national frameworks, we examine how these regulations shape the global digital landscape, influence cross-border data flows, and impact international trade.

Geopolitics of Internet Governance and Digital Sovereignty

Internet governance has become a battleground for competing geopolitical interests. In this section, we explore the geopolitics of internet governance and its relationship with digital sovereignty. From debates over internet censorship to the establishment of national firewalls, we analyze how geopolitical considerations shape the digital realm and influence global trade dynamics.

Economic Implications of Digital Sovereignty in International Trade

Digital sovereignty has significant economic implications for international trade. In this chapter, we examine how trade barriers and protectionism in the digital age impact global commerce. From the rise of national champions to the emergence of digital trade restrictions, we assess the potential consequences of these policies on economic growth, innovation, and competitiveness.

Privacy and Surveillance in the Context of Digital Sovereignty

In the pursuit of digital sovereignty, governments often grapple with the delicate balance between privacy and surveillance. We delve into the ethical considerations surrounding privacy and surveillance in the context of digital sovereignty. From the tension between national security and individual rights to the impact on cross-border data flows, we explore the challenges that policymakers face in safeguarding privacy while securing their digital domains.

Digital Sovereignty and the Future of Cloud Computing

The rise of digital sovereignty has raised questions about the future of cloud computing. In this section, we analyze how digital sovereignty shapes the landscape of cloud computing. From the development of national cloud infrastructures to concerns over data localization, we explore the implications of these policies on the future of cloud computing and the potential disruptions to global data flows.

Cultural Preservation and Digital Sovereignty

Digital sovereignty has profound implications for cultural preservation. In this chapter, we examine how nations seek to preserve their cultural heritage in the digital age. From content filtering to the development of national digital libraries, we explore the tensions between cultural preservation and the open nature of the internet, shedding light on the challenges faced by policymakers in maintaining cultural sovereignty.

Digital Sovereignty and the Role of Artificial Intelligence

Artificial intelligence (AI) has emerged as a transformative technology with implications for digital sovereignty. We explore how AI intersects with digital sovereignty, from the development of national AI strategies to concerns over data ownership and control. We analyze how countries are positioning themselves in the global AI race and the implications for international trade and technological leadership.

Digital Rights and Digital Sovereignty

The pursuit of digital sovereignty raises important questions about digital rights. In this section, we examine how digital sovereignty intersects with human rights, freedom of expression, and access to information. From internet censorship to restrictions on online platforms, we explore the tensions between digital sovereignty and the protection of fundamental rights, offering insights into the ethical considerations at stake.

Ethical Considerations in the Battles for Digital Sovereignty

The battles for digital sovereignty raise a multitude of ethical considerations. In this chapter, we delve into the ethical implications of trade barriers and protectionism in the digital age. From the potential for digital divides to the impact on global collaboration and innovation, we explore the ethical dilemmas faced by policymakers, legislators, scholars, educators, and the public as they navigate the complex landscape of digital sovereignty.

In conclusion, this subchapter sheds light on the challenges and implications of trade barriers and protectionism in the digital age. Addressing a diverse audience of politicians, legislators, scholars, educators, and the public, we explore the multifaceted dimensions of digital sovereignty and its impact on international trade, cybersecurity, privacy, cultural preservation, artificial intelligence, digital rights, and ethics. By examining these issues, we aim to foster a deeper understanding of the complexities surrounding the pursuit of digital sovereignty in our interconnected world.

Strategies for Promoting Global Digital Trade Cooperation

In today's interconnected world, digital trade has become a vital component of the global economy. However, with the rise of digital sovereignty and the battles for control over the internet, it is crucial to develop strategies for promoting global digital trade cooperation. This subchapter aims to address the challenges and provide recommendations to politicians, legislators, scholars, educators, and the public on how to foster a collaborative environment for global digital trade.

One strategy for promoting global digital trade cooperation is the establishment of international standards and norms. Policymakers and legislators should work together to develop a framework that ensures a level playing field for all participants in the digital trade ecosystem. This includes harmonizing data protection regulations, cybersecurity standards, and intellectual property rights across borders. By creating a common set of rules, countries can facilitate the flow of data and encourage cross-border trade.

Another strategy is to enhance international cooperation on cybersecurity. Cyber threats are transnational in nature and require a collective response. Governments, academia, industry, and civil society should collaborate to share information, best practices, and intelligence on cyber threats. This can be achieved through the establishment of international platforms for information exchange and capacity building programs. By working together, countries can strengthen their cybersecurity defenses and protect their digital trade infrastructure.

Furthermore, promoting digital literacy and education is essential for fostering global digital trade cooperation. Governments should invest in educational programs that equip individuals with the skills and knowledge needed to participate in the digital economy. This includes training programs on data privacy, online security, and digital entrepreneurship. A digitally literate workforce will not only contribute to the growth of the digital trade sector but also ensure that individuals are aware of their rights and responsibilities in the online world.

Lastly, it is crucial to address the geopolitical implications of internet governance and digital sovereignty. Global cooperation and dialogue are necessary to resolve conflicts and reach consensus on issues such as data localization, cross-border data flows, and access to digital services. Diplomatic efforts should focus on finding common ground and building trust between nations. Multilateral forums and international organizations can play a significant role in facilitating these discussions and promoting cooperation.

In conclusion, promoting global digital trade cooperation requires a multi-faceted approach. By establishing international standards, enhancing cybersecurity cooperation, investing in digital literacy, and addressing geopolitical challenges, governments and stakeholders can create an environment conducive to the growth of digital trade. Only through collaboration and cooperation can we secure the connected world and ensure the benefits of digital sovereignty are realized while maintaining a global digital trade ecosystem that is open, secure, and inclusive.

Chapter 6: Privacy and Surveillance in the Context of Digital Sovereignty

Balancing Citizens' Privacy Rights and National Security

In the age of digital sovereignty, the battle for securing the connected world has brought to the forefront the delicate task of balancing citizens' privacy rights with the imperative of national security. This subchapter explores the complex interplay between these two crucial aspects and delves into the ethical, legal, and technological considerations that policymakers, legislators, scholars, educators, and the public must grapple with.

The rapid advancement of technology, alongside the increasing interconnectedness of our societies, has necessitated a reevaluation of traditional notions of privacy and security. While citizens have a fundamental right to privacy, governments have a duty to safeguard their nations from cyber threats and ensure public safety. Striking the right equilibrium between these competing interests is paramount to maintain trust in the digital era.

One avenue through which this balance can be achieved is the implementation of national data protection regulations. These regulations, rooted in the principles of digital sovereignty, provide a legal framework for safeguarding citizens' personal information while enabling effective cybersecurity measures. However, finding the right balance is a complex task, as overly stringent regulations may impede innovation and hamper economic growth.

Moreover, the geopolitics of internet governance play a significant role in shaping the privacy-security dynamic. Governments must navigate the delicate terrain of international relations to establish effective cooperation mechanisms for addressing cyber threats while respecting citizens' privacy rights. Collaborative efforts, such as the development of international norms and agreements on cybersecurity, can help strike the right balance and foster trust among nations.

The economic implications of digital sovereignty in international trade cannot be overlooked. As countries increasingly assert their digital sovereignty, concerns arise regarding the potential fragmentation of the internet and its impact on global commerce. Policymakers must carefully weigh the benefits of protecting national interests against the potential adverse effects on cross-border data flows and international trade.

Furthermore, privacy and surveillance in the context of digital sovereignty raise pressing concerns. While governments must have the necessary tools to prevent and investigate criminal activities, the indiscriminate surveillance of citizens poses a threat to privacy rights. Striking the right balance between targeted surveillance and preserving civil liberties is a delicate task that requires transparent legal frameworks and robust oversight mechanisms.

As artificial intelligence (AI) plays an increasingly influential role in our societies, the intersection of digital sovereignty and AI ethics becomes crucial. Policymakers must grapple with questions of accountability, transparency, and bias in AI systems, ensuring that citizens' privacy rights are protected while harnessing the potential of AI for national security purposes.

In conclusion, the subchapter "Balancing Citizens' Privacy Rights and National Security" highlights the multifaceted challenges of striking the delicate balance between privacy and security in the age of digital sovereignty. Policymakers, legislators, scholars, educators, and the public must engage in thoughtful and inclusive discussions to develop robust frameworks that protect citizens' privacy rights while safeguarding national security in an interconnected world.

Surveillance Technologies and Their Implications

In this subchapter, we explore the various surveillance technologies that have emerged in our increasingly connected world and the implications they have on individuals, societies, and nations. As the battles for digital sovereignty intensify, it is crucial for politicians, legislators, scholars, educators, and the public to understand the profound impact surveillance technologies can have on privacy, security, and human rights.

Surveillance technologies have evolved significantly in recent years, offering powerful capabilities to governments, corporations, and even individuals. From CCTV cameras and facial recognition systems to data collection through smartphones and social media platforms, these technologies have the potential to fundamentally alter our everyday lives.

One of the key implications of surveillance technologies is the erosion of privacy. As governments and corporations collect vast amounts of data about individuals, questions arise regarding the appropriate and ethical use of this information. Striking a balance between security and privacy becomes increasingly challenging as surveillance technologies become more pervasive and sophisticated.

Furthermore, the use of surveillance technologies raises concerns about the abuse of power and the violation of human rights. Without proper regulations and oversight, these technologies can be used to target and suppress dissent, infringing upon freedom of speech and expression. The potential for mass surveillance also threatens the principles of democracy and individual autonomy.

In the context of digital sovereignty, surveillance technologies pose unique challenges. National data protection regulations become essential to safeguard citizens' privacy and ensure their digital sovereignty.

However, balancing these regulations with the needs of law enforcement and national security agencies is a delicate task.

The economic implications of digital sovereignty in international trade also come into play. Governments and businesses must navigate the tension between protecting their citizens' data and participating in global trade and innovation. Striking the right balance is crucial for fostering innovation, economic growth, and maintaining a competitive edge in the digital age.

Lastly, surveillance technologies raise important ethical considerations. As artificial intelligence and machine learning algorithms power these technologies, questions arise about bias, discrimination, and the potential for automated decision-making without human oversight. Ensuring that ethical principles guide the development and deployment of surveillance technologies is paramount.

In conclusion, surveillance technologies have far-reaching implications for individuals, societies, and nations in the age of digital sovereignty. As the battles for digital sovereignty unfold, it is crucial for policymakers, scholars, educators, and the public to understand the complexities surrounding surveillance technologies and work towards solutions that protect privacy, uphold human rights, foster innovation, and maintain a fair and just digital world.

Enhancing Privacy Protections in the Age of Digital Sovereignty

In today's interconnected world, where data flows across borders and digital technologies shape every aspect of our lives, privacy protection has become a paramount concern. The rise of digital sovereignty, the notion that nations should have control over their own digital infrastructure and data, has further complicated the landscape. In this subchapter, we will explore the challenges and opportunities in enhancing privacy protections in the age of digital sovereignty.

Privacy is a fundamental human right that must be upheld in the digital realm. As politicians, legislators, scholars, educators, and the public, it is our collective responsibility to ensure that individuals' privacy is respected and protected. National data protection regulations play a critical role in this regard. They provide a legal framework to safeguard personal data, establish consent requirements, and impose penalties for data breaches. However, in the age of digital sovereignty, a balance must be struck between protecting privacy and enabling cross-border data flows for economic and societal benefits.

The geopolitics of internet governance also intersect with privacy concerns. As nations assert their digital sovereignty, they may adopt different approaches to privacy and surveillance. It is essential to foster dialogue and collaboration to establish common frameworks that respect privacy rights while addressing national security concerns. International cooperation is crucial in harmonizing privacy regulations, promoting data sharing agreements, and combating transnational cyber threats.

Furthermore, the economic implications of digital sovereignty in international trade cannot be ignored. Privacy-enhancing technologies, such as encryption and anonymization, can foster trust and facilitate cross-border data flows. However, striking the right balance between privacy and facilitating international trade requires careful consideration. Adequate safeguards, such as data localization requirements and privacy impact assessments, must be implemented to protect individuals' privacy while enabling the free flow of data.

In the context of digital sovereignty, the future of cloud computing is also at stake. The ability to store and process data securely and privately is crucial. Governments and organizations must work together to develop secure cloud infrastructures that respect privacy rights and protect against unauthorized access.

Cultural preservation is another aspect that intersects with digital sovereignty. As nations assert control over their digital heritage, it is important to preserve cultural diversity and ensure that cultural artifacts and knowledge are not lost in the digital realm. Technological solutions can be developed to protect and preserve cultural heritage while respecting privacy rights.

Artificial intelligence (AI) plays a significant role in the battles for digital sovereignty. It has the potential to revolutionize various sectors, but also raises concerns about privacy and ethics. As AI systems become more integrated into our lives, it is crucial to establish clear guidelines and regulations to protect individuals' privacy and prevent discriminatory practices.

Digital rights in the context of digital sovereignty also need to be addressed. Individuals must have control over their personal data and be empowered to make informed decisions about its use. Access to information, freedom of expression, and the right to be forgotten are essential aspects of digital rights that must be protected.

Finally, ethical considerations must guide our battles for digital sovereignty. We must ensure that our actions and policies uphold principles of fairness, accountability, transparency, and inclusivity. Privacy protection should not be compromised in the pursuit of digital sovereignty.

In conclusion, enhancing privacy protections in the age of digital sovereignty is a complex task that requires collaboration, dialogue, and careful consideration. Balancing privacy rights with national security, economic interests, and cultural preservation is paramount. By establishing robust data protection regulations, fostering international cooperation, and integrating privacy-enhancing technologies, we can build a connected world that respects privacy and upholds human rights in the digital realm.

Chapter 7: Digital Sovereignty and the Future of Cloud Computing

The Shift Towards National Cloud Infrastructure

Title: The Shift Towards National Cloud Infrastructure

In recent years, the world has witnessed a significant shift towards national cloud infrastructure as countries strive to assert their digital sovereignty in an increasingly connected world. This subchapter explores the rationale behind this shift and its implications for various stakeholders, including politicians, legislators, scholars, educators, and the public.

With the rise of cloud computing, data has become the lifeblood of the digital economy. Recognizing the criticality of data security and privacy, many nations have started to prioritize the establishment of their own national cloud infrastructure. This move aims to ensure that sensitive data is stored and processed within the country's borders, thereby safeguarding national interests and reducing reliance on foreign cloud providers.

For politicians and legislators, understanding the dynamics of this shift is crucial in formulating national data protection regulations and digital sovereignty strategies. By promoting the development of local cloud infrastructure, governments can enhance their control over data flows, minimize the risk of surveillance by foreign entities, and strengthen their ability to protect citizen rights and national security.

Scholars and educators have a pivotal role in analyzing and disseminating knowledge about the geopolitics of internet governance and digital sovereignty. The shift towards national cloud infrastructure is deeply intertwined with these issues, as it reshapes the global digital landscape and challenges the existing power dynamics in cyberspace.

From an economic perspective, the implications of digital sovereignty in international trade are profound. While it may introduce barriers to cross-border data flows, promoting national cloud infrastructure can stimulate local innovation and job creation. However, policymakers must strike a balance between protecting national interests and fostering international cooperation to ensure a thriving global digital economy.

Privacy and surveillance concerns have become central in the context of digital sovereignty. As nations assert control over their data, they must also grapple with ethical considerations, striking a delicate balance between protecting privacy rights and enabling effective law enforcement. This subchapter delves into the complex interplay between privacy, surveillance, and digital sovereignty.

Furthermore, the future of cloud computing is intrinsically tied to digital sovereignty. As countries develop their national cloud infrastructure, they must navigate the challenges of interoperability, standardization, and technological advancements. This subchapter explores the potential benefits and risks associated with this shift and its impact on the wider adoption of cloud technologies.

Finally, this subchapter touches upon the cultural preservation aspect of digital sovereignty. As nations seek to protect their cultural heritage in the digital realm, they must consider the role of national cloud infrastructure and artificial intelligence technologies in preserving and promoting their unique cultural identities.

In conclusion, the shift towards national cloud infrastructure is a multidimensional phenomenon with far-reaching implications for various stakeholders. By delving into the intricacies of this shift, this subchapter aims to enlighten politicians, legislators, scholars, educators, and the public on the critical battles for digital sovereignty in our interconnected world.

Data Localization and Sovereign Clouds

In the era of digital sovereignty, the concept of data localization and sovereign clouds has emerged as a critical issue with far-reaching implications for individuals, businesses, and nations. This subchapter delves into the complexities surrounding this topic, exploring the various dimensions of data localization and its impact on cybersecurity, privacy, economic trade, and cultural preservation.

Data localization refers to the practice of storing and processing data within the borders of a particular country. This approach is often seen as a means to enhance national data protection regulations and strengthen digital sovereignty. However, it raises several concerns related to the free flow of information, international cooperation, and the potential fragmentation of the internet.

Sovereign clouds, on the other hand, are cloud computing platforms that are exclusively operated and controlled by a particular country or region. These platforms aim to ensure that sensitive data remains within the jurisdiction and control of the hosting nation, reducing reliance on foreign cloud service providers. However, the adoption of sovereign clouds may have significant economic implications in international trade and may disrupt the existing global cloud computing landscape.

This subchapter explores the geopolitical dynamics of internet governance and its relationship with digital sovereignty. It delves into the challenges faced by policymakers and lawmakers in balancing national interests, privacy concerns, and the need for international cooperation in cyberspace.

Moreover, it addresses the economic implications of digital sovereignty in international trade. It examines the potential impact on cross-border data flows, trade barriers, and the development of a fragmented digital economy. The chapter also highlights the importance of striking a balance between national security interests and the facilitation of global trade.

Furthermore, this subchapter examines the role of data localization and sovereign clouds in preserving cultural heritage and promoting national identity. It discusses the challenges of protecting cultural artifacts in the digital realm and emphasizes the need for digital sovereignty to safeguard cultural diversity.

Additionally, it explores the role of artificial intelligence in the battles for digital sovereignty. It analyzes the ethical considerations surrounding the development and deployment of AI technologies, emphasizing the importance of maintaining human-centric values and ensuring transparency and accountability.

Overall, this subchapter provides a comprehensive analysis of data localization and sovereign clouds, touching upon various areas of concern and their implications for cybersecurity, privacy, economy, culture, and ethics. It aims to inform and guide policymakers, legislators, scholars, educators, and the public in navigating the complex landscape of digital sovereignty and its associated challenges.

Exploring Alternatives to Traditional Cloud Computing Models

In today's interconnected world, cloud computing has become the backbone of digital infrastructure, enabling businesses, governments, and individuals to store and access data remotely. However, concerns regarding data security, privacy, and digital sovereignty have led to a growing interest in exploring alternatives to traditional cloud computing models.

One such alternative is decentralized cloud computing, which offers a more secure and privacy-centric approach to storing and processing data.

Unlike traditional cloud models where data is stored in a centralized server, decentralized cloud computing distributes data across a network of interconnected nodes. This not only enhances data security but also reduces the risk of single points of failure and potential data breaches.

Another alternative gaining traction is edge computing, which brings data processing closer to the source, reducing latency and improving efficiency. With edge computing, data is processed and analyzed at the edge of the network, on devices or servers located closer to the user. This decentralized approach reduces dependence on centralized data centers and enhances data privacy by minimizing the need to transmit sensitive information to remote servers.

Additionally, the concept of fog computing has emerged as a promising alternative to traditional cloud models. Fog computing combines the benefits of cloud and edge computing by extending the cloud's capabilities to the edge of the network. This enables real-time processing and analysis of data, reducing latency and enhancing privacy while also leveraging the scalability and resources of the cloud.

Moreover, the rise of blockchain technology has opened new possibilities for secure and decentralized data storage. Blockchain, the underlying technology behind cryptocurrencies like Bitcoin, offers a transparent and immutable ledger that can be utilized for storing and verifying data. By leveraging blockchain, organizations can ensure data integrity, enhance security, and reduce reliance on centralized cloud providers.

As policymakers, legislators, scholars, educators, and the public explore alternatives to traditional cloud computing models, it is crucial to consider the implications for digital sovereignty. The adoption of decentralized, edge computing, fog computing, and blockchain technologies can empower individuals and nations to reclaim control over their data, protect privacy, and ensure compliance with national data protection regulations.

By embracing these alternative models, countries can strengthen their cybersecurity posture, reduce dependence on foreign cloud providers, and foster innovation in the digital realm. However, careful considerations must be given to ethical considerations, digital rights, and the preservation of cultural heritage in the battles for digital sovereignty.

In conclusion, exploring alternatives to traditional cloud computing models is essential in the age of digital sovereignty. Decentralized cloud computing, edge computing, fog computing, and blockchain technology offer promising solutions that prioritize data security, privacy, and national sovereignty. By embracing these alternatives, nations can navigate the complex landscape of cybersecurity, uphold digital rights, and pave the way for a more secure and connected future.

Chapter 8: Cultural Preservation and Digital Sovereignty

Preserving Cultural Heritage in the Digital Era

In the age of digital sovereignty, the preservation of cultural heritage has emerged as a critical concern. With the rapid advancement of technology and the increasing digitization of information, it is imperative that we take steps to protect and safeguard our cultural heritage for future generations. This subchapter explores the challenges and opportunities associated with preserving cultural heritage in the digital era and highlights the importance of digital sovereignty in this context.

Cultural heritage encompasses a wide range of artifacts, monuments, traditions, and knowledge that define a society's identity. However, these valuable assets are not immune to the risks posed by the digital age. Cyberattacks, data breaches, and unauthorized access can lead to the loss or destruction of cultural heritage. Moreover, the digital era has also brought about the erosion of cultural diversity, as global connectivity and mass media tend to homogenize cultures.

To address these challenges, it is crucial for politicians, legislators, scholars, educators, and the public to recognize the significance of preserving cultural heritage in the digital era. National data protection regulations and digital sovereignty play a vital role in safeguarding cultural heritage. By enacting robust data protection laws and ensuring digital sovereignty, governments can protect valuable cultural assets from unauthorized access and misuse.

Additionally, international cooperation and collaboration are essential in preserving cultural heritage in the digital era. Countries can work together to develop frameworks and protocols to share and preserve cultural artifacts digitally. This would enable wider access to cultural heritage while ensuring its protection and integrity.

Furthermore, the use of artificial intelligence (AI) can aid in the preservation of cultural heritage. AI technologies can help digitize and analyze vast amounts of cultural data, enabling researchers and scholars to gain valuable insights into our collective heritage. However, ethical considerations must be taken into account when deploying AI in this context to ensure the protection of cultural rights and privacy.

In conclusion, preserving cultural heritage in the digital era is an important endeavor that requires the attention and commitment of politicians, legislators, scholars, educators, and the public. Through the implementation of robust data protection regulations, digital sovereignty, international cooperation, and the ethical use of technologies like AI, we can ensure the safeguarding of our cultural heritage for future generations. By embracing the principles of digital sovereignty, we can strike a balance between connectivity and the preservation of cultural diversity, fostering a world where cultural heritage thrives in the digital age.

Challenges in Protecting Cultural Sovereignty

In the age of digital sovereignty, one of the most significant challenges we face is protecting our cultural sovereignty. As the world becomes increasingly connected, our cultural heritage is at risk of being diluted, commoditized, or even erased. It is crucial for politicians, legislators, scholars, educators, and the public to understand the importance of preserving our cultural identity and the challenges we face in doing so.

One of the primary challenges in protecting cultural sovereignty is the rapid digitalization of cultural artifacts and traditions. With the advent of the internet, anyone can access and reproduce cultural content, often without the necessary context or permission. This can lead to misrepresentation, misappropriation, and the distortion of our cultural heritage. We must find ways to regulate and control the use of cultural content to ensure its integrity and authenticity.

Another challenge is the dominance of global digital platforms that often prioritize profit over cultural preservation. These platforms, such as social media networks and streaming services, have immense power in shaping and disseminating cultural content. They can easily overshadow local and indigenous cultures, leading to the homogenization of our global cultural landscape. We need to find ways to empower local communities and support their efforts in preserving and promoting their cultural heritage.

Furthermore, the rise of artificial intelligence (AI) poses both opportunities and challenges for cultural sovereignty. AI algorithms have the potential to digitize and analyze vast amounts of cultural data, allowing us to better understand and preserve our heritage. However, AI also raises concerns about the ownership and control of cultural data. We must ensure that AI technologies are used ethically and responsibly, respecting the rights and sovereignty of the communities from which the data originates.

Additionally, the economic implications of digital sovereignty in international trade can be a challenge in protecting our cultural sovereignty. Global trade agreements often prioritize economic interests over cultural preservation. We must find a balance that allows for economic growth while also safeguarding our cultural heritage.

In conclusion, protecting cultural sovereignty in the age of digitalization is a complex and multifaceted challenge. It requires a comprehensive approach that involves legislation, education, technological innovation, and international cooperation. By understanding the challenges we face and working together, we can ensure that our cultural heritage remains vibrant, diverse, and protected for future generations.

Promoting Cultural Diversity in the Connected World

In today's interconnected world, where digital technologies have become an integral part of our daily lives, promoting cultural diversity is more important than ever. With the rise of globalization and the internet, it has become easier for cultures to interact and exchange ideas, but it has also brought challenges to the preservation and promotion of cultural diversity. In this subchapter, we will explore the role of digital sovereignty in promoting cultural diversity and the various ways in which policymakers, scholars, educators, and the public can contribute to this effort.

Cultural diversity is a fundamental aspect of human civilization, encompassing the richness and uniqueness of different societies, languages, traditions, and beliefs. However, in the age of digital sovereignty, there is a risk of cultural homogenization, where dominant cultures and platforms overshadow smaller, marginalized ones. To counter this, it is crucial to establish policies that prioritize the preservation and promotion of cultural diversity.

One way to achieve this is through the development of national data protection regulations that safeguard cultural heritage. By implementing robust data protection laws, governments can ensure that cultural artifacts, traditional knowledge, and indigenous practices are not exploited or misappropriated in the digital realm. Additionally, these regulations can provide a framework for the responsible use and sharing of cultural content, striking a balance between accessibility and protection.

Moreover, educators play a vital role in promoting cultural diversity in the connected world. By integrating cultural diversity in educational curricula, educators can foster an understanding and appreciation of different cultures among students. This can be done through the inclusion of diverse perspectives in textbooks, teaching materials, and classroom discussions. By nurturing cultural sensitivity and empathy, educators can empower the next generation to become global citizens who value and respect cultural diversity.

Scholars and researchers can contribute to the promotion of cultural diversity by studying the impact of digital technologies on cultural preservation and dissemination. By conducting interdisciplinary research, they can identify innovative ways to leverage digital tools and platforms to safeguard cultural heritage and promote cross-cultural dialogue. This research can inform policymakers and practitioners in their efforts to create inclusive digital environments that celebrate and protect cultural diversity.

In conclusion, promoting cultural diversity in the connected world requires a multi-faceted approach involving policymakers, legislators, scholars, educators, and the public. Through the development of national data protection regulations, integration of cultural diversity in education, and interdisciplinary research, we can ensure that the digital world becomes a platform for cultural exchange and understanding rather than a source of cultural homogenization. By embracing cultural diversity, we can harness the power of digital technologies to create a more inclusive and interconnected global society.

Chapter 9: Digital Sovereignty and the Role of Artificial Intelligence

Harnessing AI for National Security

In the age of digital sovereignty, the role of artificial intelligence (AI) in national security has become increasingly important. AI has the potential to revolutionize the way nations protect their citizens, defend against cyber threats, and maintain sovereignty in the digital realm. This subchapter explores the implications and opportunities of harnessing AI for national security.

AI technologies offer unique advantages in the realm of national security. Machine learning algorithms can analyze vast amounts of data and detect patterns that may be imperceptible to human analysts. This capability enables early detection of cyber threats, rapid response to attacks, and improved decision-making in crisis situations. AI-powered surveillance systems can also enhance border security, identify potential threats, and protect critical infrastructure.

However, the integration of AI in national security also raises ethical considerations. The use of AI for surveillance, for example, may infringe on individual privacy rights if not properly regulated. Striking the right balance between security and privacy is crucial to maintain public trust and ensure the responsible use of AI technologies.

Moreover, ensuring digital sovereignty in the context of AI requires robust national data protection regulations. Nations must establish frameworks that safeguard their citizens' data from unauthorized access or exploitation by foreign entities. This includes developing secure data storage infrastructure, implementing encryption standards, and fostering domestic AI research and development capabilities.

The economic implications of digital sovereignty in international trade cannot be overlooked. Nations that effectively leverage AI for national security gain a competitive advantage in the global market. However, this advantage must be balanced with international cooperation and adherence to ethical guidelines to prevent the weaponization of AI and maintain stability in the international system.

In conclusion, the harnessing of AI for national security presents both opportunities and challenges in the age of digital sovereignty. Politicians, legislators, scholars, educators, and the public must work together to establish robust national data protection regulations, address ethical considerations, and foster domestic AI capabilities. By doing so, nations can ensure their citizens' safety, defend against cyber threats, and maintain sovereignty in the interconnected world.

Ethical Considerations in AI Development

Artificial Intelligence (AI) is rapidly transforming various aspects of our lives, from healthcare and transportation to finance and entertainment. As we embrace the potential benefits of AI, it is crucial to consider the ethical implications that arise from its development. This subchapter will delve into the ethical considerations in AI development, examining the challenges and opportunities it presents in the context of digital sovereignty.

AI technology has the power to significantly impact society, raising concerns about privacy, bias, accountability, and transparency. Policymakers, legislators, scholars, educators, and the general public must grapple with these ethical considerations to ensure the responsible and equitable development and deployment of AI systems.

One key ethical consideration is privacy and surveillance. AI systems, such as facial recognition and predictive algorithms, can collect vast amounts of personal data, raising concerns about surveillance and potential misuse. Striking a balance between the need for security and privacy rights is crucial to protect individuals' fundamental rights while harnessing the benefits of AI.

Another ethical concern is the potential for bias in AI algorithms. If not properly designed and tested, AI systems can perpetuate existing biases and inequalities, leading to unfair outcomes. Policymakers and developers must address this issue by ensuring diversity and inclusivity in the development process and regularly auditing AI systems for bias.

Accountability and transparency are also vital ethical considerations. AI systems often operate as "black boxes," making it challenging to understand how decisions are made. Establishing mechanisms for accountability, including explainability and audits, is crucial to ensure that AI systems are fair, accountable, and transparent.

Moreover, ethical considerations extend to the economic implications of digital sovereignty in international trade. As nations assert their digital sovereignty, questions arise about the impact on global trade and technological advancements. Policymakers must strike a balance between protecting national interests and fostering international collaboration to prevent fragmentation and promote innovation.

Cultural preservation is another critical aspect of AI development. As AI algorithms shape our digital experiences, there is a risk of homogenization and erosion of cultural diversity. Policymakers and stakeholders must ensure that AI systems respect and preserve cultural heritage while promoting innovation and creativity.

Finally, digital rights and digital sovereignty intersect in the realm of AI development. Protecting individuals' digital rights, including privacy, freedom of speech, and access to information, is essential in the age of AI. Policymakers must navigate the complex landscape of digital sovereignty while upholding democratic values and protecting human rights.

In conclusion, the ethical considerations in AI development are of paramount importance in the battles for digital sovereignty. By addressing privacy, bias, accountability, transparency, economic implications, cultural preservation, digital rights, and more, policymakers, legislators, scholars, educators, and the public can collectively shape a responsible and equitable AI future. By ensuring that AI systems are developed and deployed with ethical considerations in mind, we can harness the transformative potential of AI while safeguarding our values and societal well-being.

The Future of AI and Digital Sovereignty

Artificial Intelligence (AI) is rapidly transforming our world, and its future implications for digital sovereignty cannot be ignored. As we navigate the new frontiers of battles for digital sovereignty in a connected world, it is crucial for politicians, legislators, scholars, educators, and the public to understand the profound impact of AI and its intersection with our digital sovereignty.

One of the key aspects to consider is the role of AI in national data protection regulations and digital sovereignty. As AI technologies become more advanced, ensuring the security and privacy of citizens' data becomes increasingly challenging. Policymakers need to establish robust frameworks and regulations that balance the benefits of AI with the protection of individual rights and national security.

Moreover, the geopolitics of internet governance and digital sovereignty are closely intertwined with the development of AI. The race for dominance in AI technologies has become a battleground for nations, with implications for economic power and national security. It is imperative for policymakers to understand the geopolitical implications and work towards fostering international cooperation and collaboration in AI research and development.

The economic implications of digital sovereignty in international trade cannot be underestimated either. As AI becomes a driving force in global economies, countries must strike a balance between protecting their domestic industries and fostering international trade. Policymakers need to ensure that regulations and policies support innovation and competitiveness while safeguarding national interests.

The future of cloud computing is also intricately linked to digital sovereignty. As AI relies heavily on cloud infrastructure, countries must evaluate the risks and benefits of relying on foreign cloud providers. Developing indigenous cloud capabilities can enhance national security, data privacy, and control over critical infrastructure.

Cultural preservation is another important aspect of digital sovereignty. As AI algorithms become more prevalent in shaping our cultural experiences, policymakers need to address concerns around cultural homogenization and the protection of cultural diversity. Balancing technological advancements with cultural preservation is crucial to maintain a sense of cultural identity in the digital age.

Ethical considerations in the battles for digital sovereignty cannot be overlooked either. Policymakers must ensure that AI technologies are developed and deployed ethically, respecting human rights, privacy, and societal values. Establishing ethical guidelines and regulatory frameworks will be essential to prevent the misuse of AI and protect individuals' rights.

In conclusion, the future of AI and digital sovereignty is a complex and multifaceted topic that requires careful consideration from politicians, legislators, scholars, educators, and the public. By understanding the implications of AI on national data protection, geopolitics, economy, privacy, cultural preservation, ethics, and digital rights, we can work towards securing a connected world where AI and digital sovereignty coexist harmoniously.

Chapter 10: Digital Rights and Digital Sovereignty

Balancing Digital Rights and National Interests

In today's interconnected world, the battle for digital sovereignty has become increasingly complex, with governments, corporations, and individuals grappling with the delicate balance between protecting digital rights and safeguarding national interests. As we navigate this new terrain, it is crucial to examine the various dimensions and implications of this struggle.

National data protection regulations and digital sovereignty have become central to the conversations surrounding cybersecurity. Governments are enacting laws and regulations to protect their citizens' data from breaches and cyber threats. However, these regulations must be carefully crafted to ensure that they do not impede the free flow of information or infringe upon individual digital rights. Striking the right balance is vital to maintain the integrity of both national interests and individual liberties.

The geopolitics of internet governance and digital sovereignty further complicate this landscape. As global powers vie for control over cyberspace, the debates surrounding who should govern the internet and how it should be regulated intensify. It is crucial for policymakers, legislators, and scholars to engage in constructive dialogues to establish frameworks that respect national interests while upholding the principles of an open and free internet.

The economic implications of digital sovereignty in international trade cannot be ignored. As countries seek to protect their digital industries, concerns about data localization and restrictions on cross-border data flows arise. Striking the right balance between protecting national interests and fostering international trade and innovation is essential to sustain economic growth and prosperity in the digital age.

Privacy and surveillance are also critical aspects of the digital sovereignty discourse. Governments must navigate the fine line between ensuring national security and respecting individuals' right to privacy. Transparent legal frameworks and robust oversight mechanisms are necessary to strike an appropriate balance that protects both security and privacy.

The future of cloud computing is another frontier where digital sovereignty comes into play. As governments prioritize data sovereignty, questions arise about the implications for multinational cloud service providers and their ability to operate across borders. Finding common ground on issues of data storage, access, and control will be crucial in shaping the future of cloud computing.

Cultural preservation is another significant consideration in the battles for digital sovereignty. As governments strive to protect and promote their cultural heritage in the digital realm, questions of ownership, access, and preservation emerge. Balancing the preservation of cultural diversity with the principles of an open and global internet is a complex challenge.

The role of artificial intelligence (AI) in digital sovereignty is also a topic of great significance. As AI technologies advance, questions arise about who controls AI systems and how they are governed. Striking a balance between fostering innovation and ensuring ethical considerations in AI development is crucial to prevent the concentration of power and protect individual rights.

Finally, digital rights must be at the forefront of discussions surrounding digital sovereignty. Governments and policymakers must recognize and uphold the fundamental rights of individuals in the digital realm, including freedom of expression, access to information, and protection against discrimination. Balancing these rights with national interests is essential to ensure a fair and equitable digital landscape.

In conclusion, the battles for digital sovereignty require careful consideration of the delicate balance between protecting digital rights and safeguarding national interests. Policymakers, legislators, scholars, educators, and the public must engage in thoughtful dialogues to navigate this complex terrain. By striking the right balance, we can secure a connected world that respects both individual liberties and national security.

Ensuring Human Rights in the Digital Age

In an increasingly interconnected world, the protection of human rights in the digital age has become a paramount concern. As technology continues to evolve and shape our societies, it is crucial for policymakers, scholars, educators, and the public to understand the importance of safeguarding human rights in this new era.

The advent of the internet and the rise of digital sovereignty have brought about a myriad of challenges and opportunities. While the digital world offers immense potential for economic growth, innovation, and global collaboration, it also poses significant risks to individual privacy, freedom of expression, and other fundamental human rights.

One of the key aspects that needs to be addressed is the development of national data protection regulations in line with the principles of digital sovereignty. Governments and policymakers must work together to establish robust frameworks that ensure the privacy and security of individuals' personal data. These regulations should be designed to protect citizens from both domestic and foreign threats, while also fostering an environment that promotes innovation and economic growth.

Moreover, the geopolitics of internet governance and digital sovereignty are critical factors to consider. As countries vie for control over the internet and seek to assert their influence, it is important to strike a balance between national security interests and the principles of an open and free internet. Efforts should be made to promote multistakeholder models of governance that involve governments, civil society organizations, businesses, and individuals in decision-making processes.

In the context of digital sovereignty, the economic implications cannot be overlooked. International trade and commerce increasingly rely on digital platforms, and it is crucial to ensure that countries can protect their economic interests without compromising human rights. Striking the right balance between economic competitiveness and the protection of individual rights is vital for achieving sustainable and inclusive growth in the digital age.

Furthermore, the issue of privacy and surveillance in the context of digital sovereignty requires careful consideration. Governments must establish clear guidelines and safeguards to prevent excessive surveillance while ensuring national security. Transparency and accountability in the use of surveillance technologies are essential to maintain public trust and confidence.

Cultural preservation also emerges as a vital aspect of digital sovereignty. As the digital age transforms the way we create, consume, and share cultural content, it is important to protect and preserve diverse cultural expressions. Efforts should be made to promote digital sovereignty in a way that respects and celebrates cultural diversity, ensuring that all communities have equal opportunities to participate and benefit from the digital world.

Artificial intelligence (AI) and its role in the battles for digital sovereignty require ethical considerations. As AI becomes increasingly integrated into our daily lives, it is essential to ensure that AI systems are developed and used in ways that respect human rights and ethical principles. Governments and policymakers must establish clear guidelines and regulations to prevent discriminatory algorithms, biased decision-making, and other potential human rights violations.

In conclusion, ensuring human rights in the digital age is an urgent task that requires the collaboration of politicians, legislators, scholars, educators, and the public. By addressing issues such as national data protection regulations, internet governance, economic implications, privacy, surveillance, cultural preservation, AI, and digital rights, we can create a secure and inclusive digital environment that upholds human rights and promotes the well-being of individuals and societies worldwide.

Strengthening Legal Frameworks for Digital Rights Protection

In today's interconnected world, the protection of digital rights has become a critical issue that demands immediate attention from policymakers, legislators, scholars, educators, and the public at large. As we navigate the complex landscape of the digital age, it is essential to establish robust legal frameworks that safeguard our fundamental rights and freedoms in the digital realm. This subchapter delves into the importance of strengthening these legal frameworks to ensure the protection of digital rights in the age of digital sovereignty.

Digital sovereignty, as a concept, encompasses the ability of nations to exercise control over their digital infrastructure, data, and online activities. However, this sovereignty should not come at the expense of individual rights and freedoms. It is therefore crucial to strike a delicate balance between national security concerns and the protection of civil liberties in the digital realm.

One way to achieve this delicate balance is by enacting comprehensive national data protection regulations. These regulations should not only focus on safeguarding personal information but should also address emerging issues such as data breaches, identity theft, and online harassment. By implementing stringent data protection measures, governments can promote trust and confidence in the digital ecosystem, thereby fostering a secure and inclusive digital society.

Furthermore, strengthening the legal frameworks for digital rights protection requires a deeper understanding of the geopolitics of internet governance. As the internet transcends national boundaries, it is imperative to establish international norms and standards that promote a free, open, and secure digital environment. This subchapter explores the challenges and opportunities associated with digital sovereignty in the context of internet governance, emphasizing the need for global cooperation and collaboration.

Additionally, the economic implications of digital sovereignty in international trade cannot be overlooked. As countries strive to protect their digital assets, it is crucial to strike a balance between safeguarding national interests and fostering global economic growth. This subchapter examines the potential trade-offs and explores strategies for promoting digital sovereignty without stifling innovation and impeding cross-border digital trade.

In conclusion, strengthening legal frameworks for digital rights protection is a multifaceted task that requires the collective effort of politicians, legislators, scholars, educators, and the public. By addressing the key issues highlighted in this subchapter, we can pave the way for a secure and inclusive digital future, where individual rights and freedoms are respected, and digital sovereignty is upheld.

Chapter 11: Ethical Considerations in the Battles for Digital Sovereignty

Ethical Implications of Digital Sovereignty Policies

In the rapidly evolving landscape of cyberspace, the concept of digital sovereignty has emerged as a critical issue with far-reaching ethical implications. As governments and organizations across the globe strive to assert control over their digital domains, questions of privacy, surveillance, and the protection of individual rights have come to the forefront. This subchapter explores the ethical considerations inherent in the battles for digital sovereignty, addressing the concerns of politicians, legislators, scholars, educators, and the general public.

One of the primary ethical concerns surrounding digital sovereignty policies is the potential infringement on individual privacy and civil liberties. As nations implement national data protection regulations, there is a fine balance to be struck between safeguarding personal data and enabling legitimate law enforcement activities. Striking this balance requires careful consideration and collaboration between governments, technology companies, and privacy advocates to ensure that personal information is adequately protected while maintaining public safety.

Another ethical implication arises in the context of surveillance. As governments assert control over their digital domains, the potential for increased surveillance capabilities becomes a pressing concern. Balancing the need for security with the protection of individual rights and freedoms is a delicate task. Striking the right balance requires transparent oversight mechanisms, robust encryption standards, and accountability mechanisms to prevent abuse and unauthorized access to personal data.

Furthermore, digital sovereignty policies have profound implications for the future of cloud computing. As nations seek to assert control over their data infrastructure, questions of data localization, cross-border data flows, and access to cloud services arise. Striking the right balance between data sovereignty and the benefits of a connected world requires careful consideration of the economic, technological, and ethical implications. It is crucial to ensure that the benefits of cloud computing, such as scalability, cost-effectiveness, and innovation, are not compromised in the pursuit of digital sovereignty.

Additionally, the battles for digital sovereignty raise concerns about the preservation of cultural diversity and heritage. As nations assert control over their digital domains, there is a risk of homogenization and the erosion of cultural identities. Ethical considerations demand that policies promote the preservation and protection of cultural diversity, ensuring that the digital realm remains a space for the expression and celebration of all cultures.

In conclusion, the ethical implications of digital sovereignty policies are vast and complex. Striking the right balance between privacy, security, economic interests, cultural preservation, and individual rights requires a multi-stakeholder approach. Policymakers, scholars, educators, and the general public must engage in informed debates and discussions to shape ethical digital sovereignty policies that safeguard individual rights and promote a connected world that respects diversity and fosters innovation.

Ethical Decision-Making in the Age of Digital Sovereignty

In today's interconnected world, the concept of digital sovereignty has become increasingly important. As nations grapple with the challenges of protecting their citizens' data and ensuring national security, ethical decision-making has emerged as a critical component. This subchapter explores the ethical considerations that policymakers, scholars, educators, and the public must address in the context of digital sovereignty.

One of the primary ethical concerns is striking a balance between national security and individual privacy. As governments implement national data protection regulations, it is crucial to ensure that citizens' rights to privacy are respected. Policymakers must carefully consider the extent to which surveillance and data collection are necessary to safeguard national interests without infringing upon individual liberties.

Another ethical dilemma arises in the context of internet governance. The geopolitics of internet governance and digital sovereignty present challenges in ensuring a fair and inclusive global digital ecosystem. Policymakers must grapple with questions of fairness, transparency, and equal access to information, while also protecting national interests. Striking this balance requires ethical decision-making and a commitment to fostering global cooperation.

The economic implications of digital sovereignty in international trade also raise ethical questions. While protecting domestic industries and data can be seen as a form of economic defense, it is essential to consider the potential negative impact on global collaboration and innovation. Policymakers must weigh the economic benefits against the ethical implications of restricting access to international markets and stifling technological advancement.

Cultural preservation is another ethical consideration in the battles for digital sovereignty. As nations strive to protect their cultural heritage in the digital age, questions arise about the ownership and control of cultural artifacts and expressions. Policymakers must carefully navigate these ethical complexities to ensure that cultural diversity is respected and preserved while maintaining national sovereignty.

Artificial intelligence (AI) introduces yet another ethical dimension to digital sovereignty. As AI becomes increasingly integrated into society, policymakers must address issues related to accountability, transparency, and bias. Ethical decision-making is crucial in establishing guidelines and regulations that govern the deployment and use of AI technologies while safeguarding individual rights and societal values.

Digital rights are fundamental to the battles for digital sovereignty, and ethical considerations play a vital role in shaping the discourse. Policymakers, scholars, educators, and the public must actively engage in conversations surrounding privacy, freedom of expression, and access to information. Ethical decision-making is necessary to strike the right balance between protecting national interests and upholding digital rights.

In conclusion, ethical decision-making is paramount in the age of digital sovereignty. Policymakers, legislators, scholars, educators, and the public must consider the ethical implications of their actions in areas such as privacy, surveillance, internet governance, economic implications, cultural preservation, artificial intelligence, and digital rights. By engaging in thoughtful and ethical decision-making, we can navigate the complex challenges of the connected world while upholding our values and principles.

The Role of Ethics in Shaping Digital Sovereignty Policies

In the age of interconnectedness and rapid technological advancements, the concept of digital sovereignty has gained significant importance. As nations strive to protect their citizens' digital rights and interests, policymakers must consider the ethical implications of their decisions. This subchapter explores the vital role of ethics in shaping digital sovereignty policies and the impact it has on various aspects of our society.

Ethics, a set of moral principles, plays a crucial role in determining the boundaries and guidelines for a nation's digital sovereignty policies. Policymakers, while formulating regulations and laws, need to consider the ethical implications of their decisions. This involves striking a balance between protecting national interests and upholding individual rights and privacy.

One area where ethics takes center stage in digital sovereignty policies is in the context of privacy and surveillance. As governments seek to protect their citizens from cyber threats and maintain national security, they often resort to surveillance measures. However, this raises concerns about potential abuse of power and invasion of privacy. Ethical considerations require policymakers to find the right balance between security and individual privacy.

Another significant ethical consideration in digital sovereignty policies is the role of artificial intelligence (AI). As AI technologies become more integrated into our daily lives, policymakers must ensure that AI is used ethically and responsibly. This involves addressing concerns related to bias, transparency, and accountability in AI algorithms and decision-making processes.

Ethics also has a significant impact on the economic implications of digital sovereignty in international trade. When nations impose data protection regulations and restrict cross-border data flows, it can hinder global trade and economic growth. Policymakers must carefully consider the ethical implications of such restrictions and strike a balance between protecting national interests and fostering international cooperation.

Furthermore, the cultural preservation aspect of digital sovereignty also raises ethical questions. As nations strive to preserve their cultural heritage in the digital realm, policymakers need to ensure that this preservation is done ethically and with respect for the rights and interests of indigenous communities.

In conclusion, ethics plays a crucial role in shaping digital sovereignty policies. Policymakers must carefully consider the ethical implications of their decisions, especially in areas such as privacy, AI, international trade, and cultural preservation. By incorporating ethical considerations into their policies, governments can strike a balance between protecting national interests and upholding individual rights and values in the interconnected world.

Conclusion: Navigating the Complexities of Digital Sovereignty

In this book, "Securing the Connected World: Cybersecurity in the Age of Digital Sovereignty," we have explored the multifaceted concept of digital sovereignty and its implications on various aspects of our lives. Throughout the chapters, we have delved into the battles for digital sovereignty in a connected world, national data protection regulations, the geopolitics of internet governance, economic implications in international trade, privacy and surveillance, the future of cloud computing, cultural preservation, artificial intelligence, digital rights, and ethical considerations.

As politicians, legislators, scholars, educators, and members of the public, it is crucial for us to navigate the complexities of digital sovereignty to ensure the security and well-being of our societies. The challenges we face in the digital realm are intertwined with the rapid advancements in technology, which have transformed our lives in unimaginable ways. However, with these advancements come new vulnerabilities and threats that require our immediate attention.

One of the key takeaways from this book is the need for a comprehensive and collaborative approach to cybersecurity and digital sovereignty. It is no longer a matter that can be addressed solely by individual nations or organizations. Instead, it requires a global effort to establish common standards, regulations, and frameworks that can protect our digital infrastructure and ensure the privacy and security of our citizens.

Moreover, we must recognize the importance of balancing individual rights and collective interests in the battles for digital sovereignty. While protecting national interests and data is crucial, we must not undermine the fundamental rights of individuals, such as privacy and freedom of expression. Striking this balance requires careful deliberation and the involvement of all stakeholders – governments, private sector entities, civil society, and the public.

Furthermore, we must invest in education and awareness programs to empower individuals with the knowledge and skills necessary to navigate the digital landscape safely. By equipping our citizens with the necessary tools and understanding, we can foster a culture of digital responsibility, resilience, and innovation.

In conclusion, the concept of digital sovereignty poses numerous challenges in our increasingly interconnected world. However, by embracing a collaborative approach, striking a balance between individual rights and collective interests, and investing in education, we can navigate these complexities and secure the connected world. It is our collective responsibility to safeguard our digital infrastructure, protect our citizens, and ensure a prosperous future for all.